THE REASONS OF BEING PLACE

NOTHING IS A COINCIDENCE

VISHESH JOSHI

ISBN
Hardcase 979-8-89588-604-5
Paperback 979-8-89588-285-6

Contents

The Reasons of being "Place"...

"This book is specially dedicated to
Shilpa A. Kashikar (Shilpa Tai)
&
"Sangeeta Sarkar",
Swati Tai (Swati Mumma-M.D.),
Soumya Tai (Soumya Mom)

Vishesh Joshi

About this Book

7 Amazing points About the Book:

1. This book helps to know the connectivity of the Universe.
2. Helps to understand the reason behind incidents happening with us.
3. Makes us understand the Law of Karmas.
4. Helps to think on reasons for everything we are going through.
5. Short but Life changing book.
6. Best Positive feeding for your mind, while traveling.
7. Moral learning of life for children and adults too.

This is English Version. Many times in Life we think, why this has happened to us, whether we had not done anything wrong with anyone. This book will answer you. This book has 4 stories, explains the Connectivity between Universe, The Law of Karmas, and The Reasons behind everything. The stories written in this book are inspired by my own mind and life experiences. It has no relation to any event or person. If there is any resemblance to an event or person, then it will be called just a coincidence.

Thank You for Support

I would like to thank some of my special assistants after God. Some friends have helped to complete this book, some have verbally inspired me, to complete this book. I am thankful wholeheartedly to Shilpa and Swati, without whose inspiration, I would not have completed this book. At the same time, I am thankful, with my whole heart of Saumya, Akshay, Pranshant, who provided me the necessary support to complete this book. I thank to Anjali, whose support has also been valuable to me.

All these have been my inspiration in one way or other, in writing and completing this book. All these have served as motivators for me, which I needed most.

So I thank everyone wholeheartedly.

I am **thankful** to **my parents and family**.

– Vishesh Joshi (Place)

Acknowledgement/Disclaimer

The last Hindi edition of my book was good. But I have made some changes and corrections/updates in this new improvised version of my book based on readers' feedback.

Hope the changes will entertain you equally and will be successful in making the learning of stories meaningful.

The stories written in this book are inspired by my own mind and life experiences. It has no relation to any event or person. If there is any resemblance to an event or person, then it will be called just a coincidence.

– Vishesh Joshi

- Last Version Cover

Write me at: vishnovi99@gmail.com

Chapter 1

Phone Call

A call comes on Sangeeta Sarkar's cell.

"Hello"

"Hello" – Sangeeta Says.

"Sangeeta, I am Purnima speaking, can you meet me this evening?"

"Hey, what happened, why are you speaking so slowly? Everything is indeed alright?"

"Yes, let me tell you. When will you be able to meet?" – Asked by Purnima.

"I will come to your house after 6 O' clock in the evening." – Sangeeta replied.

"No, not at home, Purnima said very aggressively." "In the evening we will meet in the school garden of our colony. Let's keep the phone bye." - Saying that Purnima disconnected the phone.

Two seconds of cutting the phone, by speaking bye, Sangeeta also hung up.

"Mam Bill", the newspaper man standing in front said.

"Yes give, how much?"

"755"

"Okay"

Sangeeta took the money out of the purse and gave it to him.

The newspaper man went and she went to take a bath.

The pleasant weather of the evening. Ground of school, consider like park only. Green grass, beautiful plants. Children were running and playing with ball. Some were having food sitting with the family. Some couples were talking sweetly to each other.

And Purnima was sitting sad in one corner. The evening sun was setting down and it feels like it was taking back the smile of Purnima, along with his sunshine.

"Oh God, why are you sitting here along, what happened" – Sangeeta came suddenly and asked.

"Nothing. Please have a seat. How's going on your practices?" – asked by Purnima.

"Awesome, it is court, something happens every day here. Leave it, you say, what happened? You called me suddenly here."

"Yes, today I got a call on my phone. Calls have been coming for the last 2-3 days, from different numbers, but nobody says anything. Today I receive a call, and said, Purnima, I love you. See you in this evening at S.R. Coffee shop."

"So you went?" – Sangeeta asked.

"Are you crazy? I thought I should tell you first. First I ignored some days, but when today I receive the call so…."

"Hmmm…." – Sangeeta agreed.

"Did you try to figure out, what place is the number from?" – Sangeeta questioned.

"No, how do I know?"

"There is a website, logon on that. Do you have login on that, right? An option comes in there, of the number. Put the number in it, at least it will be known from which state." Sangeeta suggested.

"Did you tell at home?" – Sangeeta asked.

"No, I cannot tell at home, Mom-dad will have tension."

Sangeeta did not say anything.

"Okay, come on, let's eat ice cream and don't worry, whoever will he will be, we will figure out." – Sangeeta lifted her by holding her hand.

"Which ice cream will you eat?"

"Whatever you feed."

"Choco bar?"

"You like that one only. Let's go."

Both leave from there.

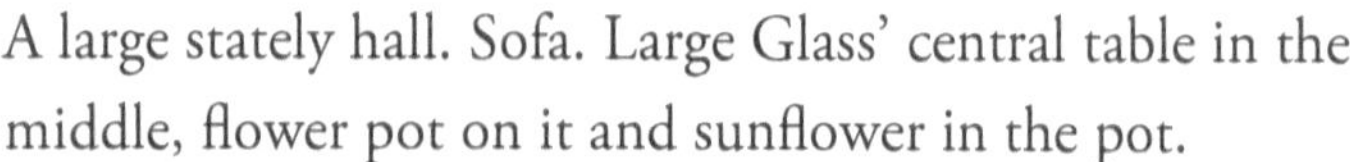

A large stately hall. Sofa. Large Glass' central table in the middle, flower pot on it and sunflower in the pot.

The gate that opened only with the security code and curtains and windows were handled by remote systems. Lights, Television, A.C., Fans, everything operates remotely. Like a smart house. Just your mobile has to be kept along with, so that everything inside the house can be handled from outside.

There are 5 securities cameras outside of house, 4 cameras in the hall and 2-2 cameras set in the every room of house.

Suddenly the door opens.... A man comes in singing a song.

"Hey, did you come?" – Aarti asked.

"Yes" while kissing on the forehead and handing the bag Hannan said.

"Where is Sarkar" – Hannan asked.

"She has gone to meet to Purnima" – Aarti answered back.

"Okay. Hey, please bring a glass of cold water."

"Yes, just brought it."

"Have it, how was your day today?"

"It was good. It is court. What might happened?"

"My Sarkar has arrived." Hannan said happily while drinking water.

"Hi dad, how're you? Miss you a lot." Sangeeta asked while hugging him and kissing him on his cheek.

"I'm doing well. Where were you? How was your day today?" – Hannan asked.

"The day was good, the evening became a little difficult." – Sangeeta replied.

"Hey, what happened?" – Her mother asked.

"Nothing just like that...... Mom, please set the table, I am very hungry."

"Dad I want to talk to you after dinner."

"Yes, you will narrate all the things to your father only, not to me, right?" – Mom said in funny way by tauntingly.

"Mom, when I would need help creating something special for a special, I would surely ask you not the father." – Sangeeta said smiley.

The trio laughingly walked into the kitchen.

While holding a coffee mug in hand, at the top of balcony, looking to city. The freezing cold wind blows, which is bringing her hairs to her face again and again and she is removing them repeatedly. Standing with the hand on railing. With holding a coffee cup in her left hand.

Takes a sip from the cup of a coffee, steeped in the deep thought.

"What are you doing here?" – Hannan asked suddenly coming from back.

"Nothing dad, just like that.... Mom gone to sleep?"

"No, she is in her room, reading a book."

"Oh! Mom and her books, now she will keep waking up till late night and will then sleep while putting the book on her face."

"Yes, that might be the reason she likes to use Facebook. ha ha ha...." – Hannan said while laughing.

"Yes, indeed." – Both laughed.

"Dad, today I got the call of Purnima, someone is calling her repeatedly and ……"

"ha ha ha ha, I got you. Did she inform at her home?"

"No, she was saying that parents will have tension, but dad, it is the responsibility of the family to help to their children, if there is any problem." – Sangeeta said a little upset.

"Yes of course. You try to convince her that tell your problem at home." – Hannan said.

"Yes but…" – Sangeeta tried to speak.

"Daughter, what is this?" – Hannan asked.

"It is a cell phone." – Sangeeta answered.

"No, it is radio." – Hannan replied. "It is not a radio, but now the question is that how does it works?"

Sangeeta said – "I don't know." While uplifting her shoulders and nodding.

Hannan said – "There is a very different story behind the invention of the radio and radio waves. Albeit, later this invention expanded into the cell phones. Now, how does it works? Cell phones require the tower and little power. Mobile phones are able to send the signals in very small range, then how do we talk from one city to another?"

Several types of towers, also known as stations, it catches weak waves of mobile, and send them forward by modulating.

"I explained it to you briefly." –Hannan Said.

"But dad, why are you telling me all this?"

"Dear Daughter, consider Purnima is a cell phone, who has problems like signal and her parents are another cell phone." Hannan stops there and take a sip of coffee and then continues. "This is very strange example but try to understand. Her parents want to take the signals but Purnima is not able to send. I mean, she is not able to tell her problems to them. So, you will have to act like a tower between of them so that Purnima's issue can reach them well." - Hannan Said.

"So you want me to talk to her parents?" – Sangeeta asked in surprise and in a slightly aggressive tone.

"No, not the matter. I want that you make them feel that if the child is unable to share then there is no fault of the child. This happens due to inability to talk between the two and due to the distance between the child and the parents. Once make them realize what they have to do. Once they realized it, then their wish. And where is the will there is way." – Hannan said.

"Fine, let me see." – Sangeeta said.

"Do you know Sarkar, what we have learnt today?" – Hannan asked.

"That's how the cell phone works?" – Sangeeta answered.

"No, we have learnt that a cell phone can also help us in finding the solutions. Then we are humans."

"You're great Dad." – Sangeeta said.

"Ya, great. It got cold, considering it cold coffee, I do drink it." – Hannan said.

"Yes, mine too." – Sangeeta said.

"Come on, good night. You too sleep. It is 11:30 PM." - He turned back and said while going. He drank the coffee like the water while returning back.

Sangeeta is standing with her hand on the railing, she drank coffee like the water. Stand there only for a while, stares at the clouds crossing the moon, as if she wants to go somewhere along with them. Then she quickly turns around and goes inside.

In the morning, Purnima is reading a book while having breakfast at the dining table.

Then the cell phone rings. The book is so enjoyable to read that eyes are completely fixed on book. And without looking, she picks up the cell phone with the opposite hand.

The cell phone was kept upside down therefore, picks up the cell phone, straight it up, swipe the answer button and put it on ear while reading the book.

"Hello"

"Hello"

The phone gets disconnected. Suddenly she says being very conscious – "Oh, unknown number."

Before she thinks of anything else, the call comes again from another number. She picks up the call.

"Hello"

"Hello Purnima, I am Anjali this side."

"Anjali, Hi. Whose number is this?" – Purnima asked.

"Hey, this is my mom's number, my phone is on charging. As you already know the condition of my cell phone." – Anjali said.

"Yes, that is a box only. I know, I know. Please tell, what happened?" – Purnima said.

"Hey, you have my book with you, don't you? Have you read? Actually, I am in need of it now. May you please return it?" – Anjali said.

"Yes, yes, I have read it. Sorry my dear. I think every night that I'll return it tomorrow and then I forget. Take it in collage today, I will bring it definitely." – Purnima said.

Purnima puts the phone on table upside down, near her. Taking the last piece of bread in the mouth, she runs right away towards the book-shelf.

Lot of books are kept there in the book-shelf and a lot of dust has also formed. She takes out a book while coughing. Suddenly, a card falls down. She picks it up, turns it, smile and then keep it safe in the drawer there, cleans the book by a cloth kept nearby and approaching the dining table put it in the bag kept on a chair.

"Mom, I am going."

"Ride carefully." – Mom shouts from inside.

Purnima employs her Scotty in the collage parking lot. Scotty was still on the stand, a voice comes from behind.

"Hi Purnima, did you bring my book?" – Anjali said.

"Yes darling, I have brought it. Be a little patient. This stand….. okay done. Hi, how're you?" – Purnima asked while removing the scarf from her face.

"Yes, I am fine." – Anjali replied.

Takes out the book from Scotty's trunk and keeps it on the scarf and closes the Scotty's trunk.

"Let's come. Your book, take it." – Purnima said.

"Thanks" – Anjali said.

"That 'miss call issue', got sorted out or not?" – Anjali asked.

"No dear, I don't know who is he? Once I get him, then I ……"

"I will eat him, right?" – Anjali said while laughing in loud.

"Eat? I will….." – Purnima stops there while speaking.

Anjali pulls her left on the way of library, while holding her hand. "Hey, let's come to library. I want to gets some book issued."

Both go to library. Purnima looks at the books like seeing someone's picture in books.

"Oh Madam, why do you always look at books like this?" – Anjali said while hitting softly on her shoulder.

"Without saying anything, how much the books say to us. This is the only thing in the world that speaks without voice." – Purnima said.

"Wow, what is the matter, philosopher, these are your thoughts or that friend of yours?" – Anjali asked.

Purnima just smiles back.

"Let's not talk much here. Let's go outside."

Both get entries done of books on the counter and went outside. After going out Purnima checks the cell. Again one miss call and one message. “I want to meet you.”

Purnima angrily lock the cell’s keypad. Here Anjali is being spoken in her tune.

“When you are going to introduce me to your friend?” You always talk about her, praise her. I want to meet her too. – Anjali said.

“Okay, I will surely introduce her to you.” – Purnima replied.

Both go for the lecture.

A room full of the books, as alike not a room but a library. But it cannot be called a library because, apart from the books, a lot of things were kept there.

A large double bed in middle. A hall or a massive room, window in left side. The rest of wall is full of the book shelf itself. That hall will be at least 40x40.

Sangeeta sitting on the bed comfortably and reading the book. It is evening. 5:30 p.m. Sangeeta picks up the phone and go to last call and dials the number.

The bell is ringing.

“Hello” – Voice comes from the front.

"Hello Purnima, listen, can you come my home straight from collage?" – Sangeeta asked.

"Yes surely. Just getting out, I am in the parking lot. I will be there within 45 minutes."

"Yes, take your time." – Sangeeta hung up.

Purnima reaches Sangeeta's house. Sangeeta takes her to her room.

"Where is Aunty?" – Purnima asked.

"She has gone to temple" – Sangeeta replied.

"Take a seat please." – Sangeeta seats on bed and asked her too, to seat by near her.

"Did you come to know anything?" – Sangeeta asked.

"No dear. Today also I have received the miss calls with one message. I was in the library that time and my cell was on silent. I even don't know it was call or gave a miss call. Sangeeta, you please talk to your father, he will get the calls traced by the commissioner and will get him catch." – Purnima said everything in one breath.

Sangeeta gets up listening to her talk, raises the pot of water kept on the table near bed and says adding water to the tumbler.

"No Purnima." – says while offering the water to her.

"What?" – Asking just this, Purnima first drinks the water.

Purnima keeps the tumbler on the table, which was at the left side of her.

"Look Purnima, until we do not know, who is patient, how is he, how is his disease, it is difficult to say that to which doctor we should take him or which medicine should be prescribed." – Sangeeta said.

"When did you get the first call" – Sangeeta asked quickly.

"Before a week ago. At first, I started getting miscall. I did not pay attention, then I got call, I picked up, so he said, "I love you Purnima, I want to meet you." I asked, who is this on the line? So he disconnected the call. Then a couple of times this happened. Then I stopped picking up calls from unknown numbers. So now, I have started receiving messages that want to meet you." – Purnima said very disappointedly.

"Who all have your this number?"

"With everyone Sangeeta. This is my very old number."

"Recently, any new friend, who is suspect?"

"No, there is no one such."

"Try to remember, anyone in mutual friends, or might have shared the number in collage or on Facebook.

Is the number added to your Facebook account and being displayed? Is it?" – Sangeeta asked.

"No dear. Due to mid-sem, I did not meet many people and this number is not added or being displayed to Facebook, not even on Orkut or any other social media platform." – Purnima replied.

Sangeeta strolled in the room, asking questions.

"Have you updated the contact number in any malls or any job fairs, etc.?" – Sangeeta asked.

"No, since long time, I did not visit any fair."

"Look Purnima, the mobile numbers are not being available in phone directory, as because these all are private numbers of users. Without our or being given by service provider, these numbers can be not available to anyone. Your many friends and friends of friends are working in call center, aren't they?" – Sangeeta asked.

"I have no such friend personally but friends of friends are enough. The students who have been come from outside, they are doing part time job in call centers purpose of earning." – Purnima replied.

"Will you be agreed with me on one thing?" – Sangeeta asked.

"Yes, please say."

Sangeeta explains her everything. She understood too.

From next day onwards, Purnima started going collages just like every day.

It gets one week. Now no call comes. Purnima calls Sangeeta and tells her that, "an idea is working well. From that day, no call came."

Sangeeta says – "Now let's start Step-2."

Purnima replies – "Okay, I will do this."

On third day, as Purnima reaches the collage, again call comes.

"Darling, you did change the number and didn't tell us." Purnima gets very angry. "Who the bloody hell is there? Who are you and what do you want?"

"Just want to meet you" – Unknown caller said.

"Why do you want to meet me, do we know each other?"

"If you don't know then you will know."

"Why do you want to meet me?"

"I Love you."

"How do you love if we never met?"

"Therefore I'm saying, I want to meet you."

"Stupid, go to hell." – Purnima disconnected the call.

"Then only Anjali, Pooja arrives there, along with Shardha."

"Wow, new cell?" – Shardha asked.

"No dear, it is not new one. My handset fell into the water today, so now I have taken it out for use that cell has to give to fix."

"What is wrong, why you look so angry? All well?" – Anjali asked.

"Yes, all well. Let's go." – Purnima said.

At night, Purnima calls and tells Sangeeta the whole thing.

Sangeeta said - "Let's begin with the third step."

"Okay dear. Good night." – Purnima replied with smile.

Next day, Purnima reaches to collage. In Lunch.......

"Hey, what happened, why you are sitting so upset?" – Pooja asked.

"Nothing dear. Just like that...." – Purnima replied.

"Hey, tell me, what happened", in same time, Anjali and Shardha also come. Ashish and Rahul also come.

"Hey, see Purnima is sitting so upset and even not telling anything." – Pooja said.

"Dear, what happened?" – Rahul asked.

Purnima said changing the mood. – "This much food, is there a Bhandara today?"

"No, today is party." – Aashish said.

"What party?" – Pooja and Purnima asked together excitedly.

"Completion of one month of our hidden Rustom Rahul's Job."

"Job?" – All girls asked in one voice.

"Yes, I have got a job in call center, I have completed one month day today." – Rahul told.

Anjali said while hitting on his hand - "Now telling, why not tell since so many days."

"I thought, first let it get confirm, then I should tell everyone. But I told now and also surprise party given, isn't it?" – Rahul said happily.

Purnima looks at Rahul and puts her phone in the bag, which was kept on the table.

"Now you tell, what happened to you." – Aashish asked Purnima.

Purnima narrated about the incident of unknown caller and also told the reason behind changing the number along with cell phone. And said - "this cellphone is taken because auto recording starts as soon as the call is received. I have recorded his talk. Now if I get a call, I will complain to the police with the evidence."

Purnima gets the call again in the evening and one message also comes, written in that "I want to meet you, love is the intention and there is a promise, sweetheart."

At night, Purnima calls Sangeeta and explains the whole thing, then says – "Step-3 also completed, you please collect the list by tomorrow."

"Okay, give the list tomorrow and also the number from which calls are coming." – Sangeeta said.

After Dinner, Sangeeta goes to her dad's room.

"Dad, this is the number, get it traced."

"Got the number?" – Hannan asked.

"Yes, Purnima has messaged in the evening."

"Okay my dear, I will know tomorrow and will tell you."

"And Dad, don't forget what I had said."

"I will not forget my dear."

"Good night Dad. I love you."

"Love you too, good night."

In the morning, Sangeeta was sitting in her room, checking emails on the laptop. Prints out the mail by attaching the laptop to a nearby printer. Picks up the cell phone and make a call.

"Hello"

"Hello Purnima, I got mail. Thanks. List confirmed isn't it?" – Sangeeta asked.

"Yes, 100%" – Purnima replied.

"Okay, thanks. Carry on, talk you later. I will update you shortly." – Sangeeta said.

"Okay, I am leaving for the office. The sound comes from the hall below."

Sangeeta runs down keeping the laptop on the bed. Descending says – "Dad, see don't forget my work."

"Don't worry Honey, I'll not. I will give you complete details soon. I will message you."

In evening, Sangeeta comes from the court. Mom brings food to the room. Sangeeta is doing some work on the laptop. Mom gives her dinner plate to hold. Then only a message comes on Sangeeta's cell.

"Mom, while going please close the door."

"Yes, okay, this water is placed on the table." – Aarti said.

"Thanks mom."

Sangeeta checks the message.

After 2 days

"Mom, I am taking Scotty today, the car is at home." – Sangeeta said.

"Okay, once back, let me know how the seminar was?" – Aarti said.

"Yes, sure. Bye mom." – Sangeeta says in a loud voice from outside, turns on the Scotty and leaves.

On reaching collage, she pushes the bike of a boy from behind and says sorry to him. He says – "It's alright."

Both are going from the main gate of the collage towards the parking, in the same direction. The boy puts his bike on stand. Sangeeta walks around the parking lot and goes a little further.

The boy was just moving towards the class with his books that the police come there.

"Is your name Sameer?" – Asked by Superintendent of Police (S.P.).

"Yes" – That boy answered.

"Do you know any girl named Purnima?"

He got completely shocked.

At the same time Sangeeta comes there. "Hello Sir, how are you here?"

"Mam, how are you here? Yes, just came for some work." – S.P. replied.

"Any issue Sir?" – Sangeeta asked.

There has been a complaint against Sameer Kohali for harassing a girl by calling her.

"But he is Sameer Datta Sir. My friend, he is with me. You do one thing, go to the principal and ask, currently mid-sems are running then there will be no chance of him becoming absent. You will get the log register from the collage. You will have to go towards Block-B, going right from here then a left." – Sangeeta said.

Sameer was watching all this with surprise.

"Oh, so are you not Sameer Kohali?"

Sameer answered fearfully – "No….sir… actually… .I….."

"Okay mam, I'll take leave. Thanks for helping." – Saying this, S.P. goes away from there.

"Mam, who are you and why you……?" – Sameer got to say just that.

"I just did hit your scotty right away, isn't it? So as compensation, I saved you. But what is the matter, what happened. Why did the policy come to you?"

Sameer is so scared that he can't say anything.

Seeing him silent, Sangeeta says. "Okay, take care. By, I should leave now."

She begins to leave.

"Mam, please wait a minute." Sameer runs to Sangeeta. "Mam, I don't know who are you but today you have saved me from a great difficulty. If the policy case had happened, my entire career would have deteriorated. Don't know why you lied to them? You don't even know me." – Sameer said.

"So now you tell me who you are and what is the matter? Why did the police come to ask you that you have done something and are you really harassing any girl by calling her?"

Sameer started crying and says wiping his tears, - "Mam, I have a friend, she is always talking about a friend of hers. One day, I took out her friend's number from her cell phone and just started harassing her just for fun. But I did not know that she would take so seriously that she would complain to the police."

"Look Sameer, it is not a good thing to bother someone like this. Not even in joke and also not in friend circle. In which state of mind the front person is that time, what is going on his or her life, you even don't know, isn't it? A person does not live alone, many people are directly or indirectly connected to him or her. If there is any problem in his/her life, then it will also have an impact on his/her family and the people associated with him/her. Cellphones are made for our convenience, to reduce the distances not to create distances in relationship."

"Think when your friends and family will know that you were doing such thing and matter has reached the policy, will they talk to you, will they keep friendship, will the distances not grow between you and them?"

Sameer was listening all this intently because no one explained to him earlier like this with all the love and calmness. He started crying and grabs Sangeeta's feet while speaking sorry, I will never do this after today.

"Hey, what are you doing? Get up." – Sangeeta said.

"No mam, I was harassing by calling an unknown girl and today, an unknown girl only helped me today. I do promise that I will never call or message her after today." – Sameer said.

"No, you will call her and if she doesn't receive then you will say sorry by messaging her. You will introduce yourself and apologize for your behavior." – Sangeeta said.

"Okay mam, I will do the same what you said. But mam, who are you and why you saved me, you don't even know me?" – Sameer asked surprisingly.

"I am a lawyer and our job is to save people from punishment." – Sangeeta answered.

"Thank you mam, if you do not come on time today, what would have happened, you are saying the truth, you saved me from going to jail."

"No, not from going to jail, I said, I save people from punishment. Think, if the policy had taken you then how disgraceful your family members would be, when your friends come to know that you are doing such a work, then how will your friendship be affected? In collage, it does not take long to spread like a fire and you will be banned from sitting in the campus coming to collage. Perhaps you would have been thrown out of college and your whole career would have been ruined, isn't it a life sentence for you? I saved you from this punishment." – Sangeeta said.

Sameer is listening to Sangeeta with respect, as if have lost in ocean but still there is no fear of drowning.

Sameer is suddenly alert as Sangeeta stops "but how do you know that the policy have come to catch me?"

"No, I didn't knew, just guessed, your nervous appearance was clearly telling that there is some problem and then the SP told the whole issue in a short time." – She said.

"But why you told lie, you don't even……" – He asked.

"As I said we are lawyers, our work is to save people from punishment, where people are not wrong."

"Thank you so much. Today is the best day of my life." – Sameer said.

"Why" – Sangeeta asked.

"Today I learned the biggest lesson of life." – He said.

"What lesson?" – She asked.

"It would be better to help unknown people instead of harassing unknown people." – He replied.

"You are not unknown to me. Well I go. Right late, but you realize your mistake." – Sangeeta said.

Before that, he says or asks anything, Sangeeta leaves from there. Then he too wipes his tears and cleaning his face, he also goes away from there.

Like every day, in the evening, Sangeeta was sitting on her bed with her legs spread out, doing some work on laptop. It's 6 O'clock of the evening. The sun is setting, as if after lot of fatigue, now he wants to sleep. Then only someone comes knocking on the door of room.

"Sangeeta, may I come in?" – Hannan asked.

"Hi dad, please come in." Sangeeta said, turning and folding her legs.

"How did you come early today?" – Sangeeta asked.

"Purnima had come." – Hannan replied.

"Hi Purnima, please come." – She said.

"Hi, got your message in evening. What happened, did you know who was he? Did you catch him?"

"Yes, I tell you, take some breath at least. Have a sit." – Sangeeta replied.

Following Purnima, Aarti too brings three tumblers filled with water, placing on tray. Purnima, Sangeeta and Sangeeta's dad Hannan take water. Mom also sits there only, putting the tray down.

"How did you do all this?" – Hannan asked.

"Yes, let us know heard that how the future lawyer Sangeeta Sarkar did this?" – Aarti said.

Sangeeta descends from the bed and start telling the whole story, walking around the room.

"When Purnima told me the whole issue, for a few days I thought that there would a friend only, yet there were many questions in mind. Talking to Purnima, I got all my answers but it was necessary to find out that who he is and why he is doing all this?"

"The world is huge and today everyone has cell phone. In this country with the population of more than 100 crores, it is difficult to find out such person, who calls her daily. Therefore, shortening the world remains a way. Like this world, the social life of the people living in the world is very big and with the introduction of mobile phones and Facebook, it has increased. Many people join us in our social life, school, colleges, professionally, friends, friends of friends, closes friends. In such a situation, doubt goes on everyone."

"The phone numbers are private number and because of this, these are not present in any directories. Without giving by our or our friends, this number cannot reach anyone like this so one thing was confirmed that the caller is either the friend of Purnima or a friend of friends."

"So I asked Purnima to close the number for one week."

"Right" – Purnima said.

Sangeeta kept speaking continuously - "When she changed the number in the first step, now in the second step, I asked her to distribute new number to only few closed and trusted people only. This is how we divided the plan into the four steps."

Purnima started thinking something.

"As Purnima distribute the numbers, she again got the call within few days." – Sangeeta said.

"Oh, so why even distributed the number" – Aarti asked by interrupting Sangeeta.

"The number was given only to the closed people, whom Purnima knew well. If now call comes that means the person is among of them or is a mutual friend and the same thing happened, Purnima got a call."

"In the third step, I asked Purnima to share the handset as well as the plan of changing number, to her friends. If he or she is any of them or know who the person is, who is calling to Purnima, then he would have been a little careful surely. So either, he would change the number again or stop calling for few days. But Purnima gets a call on the new number again in the same evening."

"But now there was no need to explore the whole world and the city because now the caller was one of them or a mutual friend. Whose list Purnima had mailed to me."

"But we have taken three steps only, but you had said that plan has four steps." – Purnima asked.

"When you shared the number to me and dad shared the complete information of the person on *the basis* of the number, then I *have followed* him continuously for 2 days. Where he goes, what does he do, I *come* to know everything. And then third day, I reached to his collage by cutting his bike outside of his collage itself."

Then Sangeeta narrated whole things to three of them, whatever today happened in the collage.

"Sangeeta, you could have caught him. We had all evidence too. Then why did you do all this?" – Purnima questioned with some anger and surprise.

"Purnima, if you kill a bad person then a bad person will be definitely reduced, but if you change a bad person to a good person, then not only a bad person will be less as well as a good person will be born right from there. And society today needs good human beings." - Sangeeta answered very simply.

"And I also told to Sameer that I am a lawyer, my job is to save innocent people from punishment."

The eyes of Hannan Sarkar and Aarti Sarkar were clearly telling that they were proud of their daughter.

Suddenly Sangeeta's mom asked – "If you had to trace the number from dad itself, then why did you need to plan so much? You would have given the number to dad on *the first day* itself?"

"To find our which patient is and what type of disease is there? Mom, not every medicine works for every disease."

"The four step plan revealed that the caller is among of friends itself. He is not the unknown or *an outsider*. If someone would be an outsider, I would definitely take action against *him, but* friends should be given a chance, shouldn't we? He would have been arrested but who would make him realize his mistake? And mom, Purnima was afraid of telling her mom-dad, and without parent's support, how we could take police's help."

"And you know the police work anyway. And how many cases are happening nowadays. It is better to try at our own level before going to the police." – Said Sangeeta.

"But who was he?" – Purnima asked enthusiastically.

"He is Sameer, Anjali's boyfriend." – Sangeeta answered.

"What? Anjali's boyfriend, so did you inform her?" – Purnima asked shockingly.

"No, he himself will tell." – Sangeeta said.

Then Purnima's cell rings again and all four starts looking at the cell.

Purnima picks up the call - "Hello"

"Hello, when are you coming home, dear daughter?" – Purnima's mom asked.

"Yes, I am just leaving" – Purnima answered her mom.

"Okay, I am leaving now. Thanks a lot Sangeeta. After this case, I too learned a lot about life from you. Thank you so much dear." – Saying this Purnima gets up and holds Sangeeta's hand. I give you call reaching home." – Purnima said.

Purnima leaves from there.

"Proud of you Sangeeta" – Hannan said.

"Me too" – Mom Aarti said too.

"Thanks dad, thanks mom. Mom, please arrange the dinner, I am very hungry now."

"LOL, okay, lets come. Oh God! Its 7.40 p.m." – Mom says while looking at the clock on the wall of the room.

Everyone is sitting at dining table to eat. Sangeeta serves a "Dal" in a pot from cauldron, while talking, but much quantity of "dal" fall down.

"Hey daughter, what are you doing? Take it by spoon comfortably." – Hannan said with love.

"Today, due to the fatigue of seminar, is there more hunger Sangeeta?" – Mom asked.

"Seminar?" – Hannan asked suspiciously.

"Yes, today she had gone from scotty there was a seminar in college today." – Aarti said.

"Mom, there was no seminar." – Sangeeta said while serving the food in her plate. "I went to meet Sameer at his college."

"Oh, so why did not you tell me this in morning?" – Aarti asked to Sangeeta.

"My lovable Mom, if I would tell you, would you let me go?" – Sangeeta said with love.

All three laughed.

Like every day, today also, Sangeeta is looking to city from the balcony hold the coffee cup in hand, after the dinner, steeped in thoughts like the whole city is steeped in thoughts for her. The moonlight looks like as a small lamp in a larger room. She stares towards the clouds. Clouds are also going away as they are also returning to their home after a day's fatigue.

The cool cold air is touching Sangeeta, as it wants to hug her. Hairs are flying through the air like wind is rubbing her hairs.

Then, dad comes from back.

"So, you did not talk to her parents, right?" – Hannan said while attaching his coffee cup to Sangeeta's cup, doing cheers.

"Dad, did you see, what happened by putting the dal from big cauldron in a small pot?" – Sangeeta's question was very serious.

"Today's parents are not in such a state of mind that they can understand the problem of their children. They only know how to take tension. If anyone ever thinks positively under any condition, so this is the effect of his/her personality, not because they are parents."

"You are saying right daughter. Now I understood what you did at dinner today, now I got that why you suddenly did that?"

"Perhaps, they do not understand by your saying because, the ability to understand depends on them. But we are proud on you our daughter." – Hannan said.

It is Sunday, the morning after last night. Suddenly the doorbell rings. Sangeeta is reading a novel sitting on couch; she gets up and opens the door.

"Hey, what a surprise, you guys are here?" – Sangeeta asked surprisingly.

There is someone else also with us.

"Please come in, please." – Sangeeta said happily.

"Please have a sit." – Sangeeta insisted.

"No, we will take leave shortly. I just came here to thank you and to say sorry that because of me you and Purnima had so much trouble. Yesterday, Sameer came and told me everything. At first, I got very angry but when he told about you, so I felt when you have forgiven him, then I should also give him a chance." – Anjali said.

Sangeeta says - "There is no fault of Sameer in this. It happens in this age, but keeps in mind that it should never happen in future again."

"No dear mam, this will never happen again. And I will also teach the rest of my friends to never harass anyone, but help others as far as possible."

"Okay, we take leave now." – Anjali said.

"Hey how, have some tea-coffee." – Sangeeta instantly said.

"No, he has to go to Gym; I have to go to class. We leave. Thank you Sangeeta and Purnima and we apologies once again." – Anjali said.

Anjali and Sameer leave from there. Purnima comes closer to Sangeeta, holding her hands; bowed head and eyes, says thanks to her and hug her tightly. Both sit on couch. Just after a while, Purnima smiles spontaneously.

"What happened" – Sangeeta asked.

"Everything got resolved so quickly and well, isn't it? I am very happy because, I was much stressed." - Purnima says in slightly sad tone.

She says changing the mood a bit. – "Do you know why I smiled; I remembered one thing about this incident." While smiling Purnima starts narrating that incident to Sangeeta.

"Once, just like this, a sales man came to my house. Anjali was also with me that time. He gave his card, after giving the demo of product. After sometime I and Anjali called him and we did lot of mischief with him, teased him, just remembering that moment, laughed."

"Very bad thing, punk girl, we shouldn't do such thing, wrong thing." – Sangeeta laughs and said in slow voice.

"That's when Mom (Aarti) brings tea, so you guys drink tea and talk. I do come from market."

"Thank you Sangeeta." – With the first sip of tea, Purnima said in slightly serious tone,.

"Hey, enough. How many times you will thank me? Okay, if you want to thank me, will you do me a favor?"

"Yes, please say. I will do anything for you." – Purnima said.

"Come to my house for dinner this evening. Don't take it otherwise." – Sangeeta instantly quoted.

"Hey, there is nothing to mind it. I will come certainly." – Purnima says after drinking tea, keeping the cup of tea on the table.

"Hey, I leave now else mom will scold me again. I will come in evening. Thanks once again."

"Okay my Purni. Please take care of yourself." – Sangeeta said with smile.

All are sitting on dining table for dinner. Purnima and Sangeeta are seated face to face. At Sangeeta's neighborhood seat her father and Purnima's neighborhood seat Sangeeta's mom are seated so that the food can be served to both.

"Aunty, the food is so delicious." – Purnima said.

"Thank you Daughter. But Sangeeta has helped me a lot in making dishes today." – Aarti replied.

"Sangeeta always helps everyone. She did help me too, not only she did solve my problem but also she gave me very good lesson too in life. Forgiving people and giving them a chance to be good." – Purnima Said.

"Okay Purnima, can you tell me why this all happened?" – Sangeeta asked.

"Why happened, means, due to Sameer." – Purnima replied.

"No" – Sangeeta replied.

"Otherwise….?" – Purnima asked in surprise.

"Whenever a problem occurs in our life, we conclude by looking at current situation. We always feel that we have nothing to do with what happened. But the law of attractions says that whatever happens to us, we are only responsible for that. We ourselves attract that towards us. In the "Geeta" lord Krishna has also explained this thing as the fruit of karma and says that as you act, you will get the same result."

"Purnima, why this happened with you only, why Anjali's boyfriend was involved in this, why the whole incident affects Anjali and you?" – Sangeeta asked.

"Why?" Purnima questioned.

"Purnima, before 2 months ago from now, you had taken product demonstration from a sales man. That time you and Anjali were only at home. He gave his card so after few days, you called him and harassed him by doing such unknown and strange things. Isn't it?" – Sangeeta asked.

"Yes." – Purnima replied.

"You were in lead role in that incident and Anjali was your copartner. Therefore, now God has given you the fruit of your karma. How as you were in main lead role and Anjali supported you hence, Anjali also got the result of it. Caller was found as her boyfriend itself, who called you. That is why it had a bad impact on her life, although for a while but it had, Wasn't it?" – Sangeeta said.

Purnima was now ashamed on her actions. Now she had understood everything. Now all her anger for Sameer also went out from her mind.

After dinner, Purnima takes out a small gift from her bag and said while handed over it to Sangeeta – "Thanks Sangeeta, for your cooperation and lesson. Her eyes filled up."

Sangeeta also became a little emotional. "Hey, why this all, it was not needed Purnima."

By handed over the gift to her, Purnima hugs Sangeeta.

Sangeeta's parents blessed both of them; turning hands on their head and back.

Sangeeta requested Purnima to stay with her tonight. Purnima said, - "Yes I will but you will have to narrate any story."

Sangeeta said – "Then you go."

Both laughed.

At night, both of them were sitting comfortable on bed, in Sangeeta's room. Sangeeta was reading a book and Purnima was watching a movie on laptop. Purnima suddenly turned around and asks – "Sangeeta, why do you feel there is always some reason behind any incident?"

"I feel…… I feel because…., you wanted to listen story, wasn't it?" – Sangeeta said as well asked.

Purnima instantly says yes eagerly. Both lie down closing the laptop and book.

"I believe in it because……."

….. *And then Sangeeta starts narrating the story to Purnima and start explaining the philosophy of reasons.*

Chapter 2

Arabian Sea

"I Sangeeta Sarkar. I believe that there is always a reason behind every incident." There is a reason, without the reason not even a leaf moves on the earth. We just have to find the reason and that has to be believed, on it and on ourselves that we have not found that reason unnecessarily. There is definitely a reason (purpose) for getting that reason.

Sangeeta Continues narrating: After few days of continuous rain, the sky is clear as if the clouds have gone home after being exhausted. Little sunlight comes out. Parks are opened for children to play. A child was cycling very fast keeping a lot of food items on his small bicycle.

Then he suddenly falls on his face and all the food falls. This phenomenon seemed normal but when case study was done, it was found that drains overflowed when it rained very few days before today. The road was full. There was a house of ants under a drain. There were some good ants and some bad too. The house of bad ants was slightly lower and the house of good ants got a little higher, hence the food that they had stored in the summer, due to waterlogging gets washed away. Now the good ants have nothing to eat. Bad ants make fun of them and do not give them piece from their food. One ant says from among the good ants, “We do trust in God. We cannot get out but some arrangements will happen surely.” Due to rain they are afraid of getting carried away, so that cannot get out.

When that child falls from a bicycle, so whatever is his food, those ants are found in the drain.

But why did he fall, why he only? There were more people in the park. There were many ways to reach the ants. When the case study was done, it was found that this child was swimming in school on Saturday evening one day before. So he pushed one other child before jumping, this is caused the balance of other child. This is not a coincidence; as that child had fallen down this child also fell down on the face.

On Saturday evening a man got off his scooter to go to the doctor. His scooter broke down and he saw a mechanic nearby. He show him the scooter, the scooter got fixed. He left from there and reached the doctor’s place. The doctor was looking at the last patient. The patient comes out and he reaches there.

Now as the patient (Scooter man) had arrived so Doctor was not able to take a leave. After all it is his duty. So he looks at him. While he was looking at him, a mother reaches there with her child, who (child) was hurt due to a sudden fall down in the water, in swimming pool.

Mother says as soon as she arrives – "You are still there sir. I thought the clinic would have closed."

The doctor says – "Yes, just one last patient had come, otherwise I would have left. Clinic gets off by 8 O'clock."

She looks at the clock. It was 8:15 p.m.

The next day on Sunday evening when a doctor leaves the clinic and crosses half way his car got puncher. At the same time another car man crosses from there and he gives him lift.

Both of them become good friends in the car. It is revealed while talking that he is a doctor. So the lifter requests that – "If you can come with me to my house..... Later I will drop you at your home. My son fell from bicycle today, he is also hurt. It is also a great coincident that my wife has requested me that bring the doctor while returning and you met. If you do not mind......."

Doctor says – "Hey never mind. This is my duty." Both go home and there he looks at the child. On asking the doctor, the child tells how he fell from the bicycle in the park. The child and doctor become good friends. The child tells him that park is awesome and as it is a Monday holiday, he insists the doctor come to the park. Doctor gets considered in front of his insists and love and promises to come there on Monday along with family.

Everyone was enjoying in the park on Monday. A father is seated on a bench with his five year old child. His child gets off the bench and goes a little further. Then his father comes there and says – "Oh son, there are ants here. Let's not play here. He sits down to have dinner with his wife and one other family. Some ants got died under the child's feet. Those were the same bad ants."

"I always told Martine that there was a reason behind every incident. We just have to find and he was convinced on this. I understood this today again, when I read his morning mail."

"What was that in that email?" – Purnima asked.

Every morning when I get up, the eyes open, the roof is in front. There is A.C. It is cold. Even today the eyes are open. The front terrace is blue but not white. It is cold but better than A.C. Because today it is open sky, green trees and plants are there, didn't get such sleep till today.

Its 5 a.m. in the morning. Martine gets up. There is sea in front. Only the sea is there far and wide and light before the sun rises.

Such a beautiful view never appeared from the crowded flat of the city. Even if seen, never felt. Today it is felt up close.

Martine gets up in a short while. He is a surfer, a diver. This is one of the teams that came in search of a submerged ship. It is heard that every breath is accounted for inside the water. Martine and his team travel from the middle of the sea to the place where the ship was sunk. Martine and his team go to the middle of the sea via boat, where the ship was sunk. Martine descends under the water as well as the entire team. A team of 12 people and a maximum area of the sea are to be covered. Therefore pairs of 2-2 could not be made. Everyone had to make their own area alone. They were all connected to each other through technology and were able to send the signals to each other.

Martine found the ship, such a big ship, like a city. Martine goes inside the ship. All the stuff is filled with water. It seemed that some city had sunk in the sea. The rest also reach there soon. All the dead bodies are extracted from there. The air force and navy also come to help. Treasure, diamond, pearls are all carried out from there by loaded into ships and a box as well.

What is in that box? That is also transported but in separate ship, separated from all goods.

After a week ....

"What are you thinking" – Ms. Cherry asks Martine.

"Why did that ship sink? A ship departs Mumbai with 1200 people, A Royal ship filled with diamonds and gold just sinks away from its own destination. Nothing is theft. No goods disappeared from the ship. Nobody even got a chance to understand what happened and suddenly a ship sank in the water." – Martine says.

"So what do you think?" – Cherry asked.

"The place where the ship sank, the way it is drowned, someone drowned it in such a way like someone drowned a human being into water, to kill him. It seems that someone wanted to drown everyone. No one should be alive. But why....?" – Martine wonders.

"So let's solve this case." – Cherry asks.

"Yes sure." – Martine says.

"According to the list there were 1200 people on that ship but the dead bodies were found in that just 1191 people. This means 9 people were missing from there. There corpses are still being traced to the bottom of the sea. There was one the driver of the ship." – Martine says.

"Yes and these 9 people will help us." – Cherry says.

"How's that" – Martine asked.

"It is such that those 1191 that died will not be able to speak." – Cherry says.

Both laughed.

Cherry says – "The 9 people who are missing, may be possible any of them be alive. He or she can tell us what happened, how the things happened and why?"

"Yes." – Martine says.

Both start collecting the all information about the 9 people. About their house members, last jobs, about their lives, about their habits and they found one thing about one of those 9 people, which looks very strange. The driver of the ship had insurance done a few weeks before this trip.

"Martine, I got it. Look, he is Jack Kelly. He had insured 5 crores 1 week before boarding the ship." – Cherry said to Martine.

"But, why would a minor driver of a ship get such a big insurance? If you count 1 month amount for the premium, then it goes up to around 65,000/- rupees per month, as per the plan he has opted for. It's his salary slip, yes, and it's his bank account statement. His salary is 40,000 rupees per month." – Martine says.

"Then how he is able to pay this much premium?" – Cherry asks.

"Cherry, the main thing is that in his bank account, in the last 1, in 2 years even no other amount was deposited other than salary and as per CBI he doesn't hold any other bank account. According to his wife, he has not mortgaged the house nor is he in any debt. He did not have any illness or anyone in his family." – Martine says.

"Why do you feel so that there is some reason behind sank of this ship?" – Cherry asked.

"There is always a reason, behind everything. Cherry, without a reason, even a leaf doesn't fall, from the tree." – Martine says.

"But it may be possible that we are thinking too much, there would nothing like that." – Cherry says.

Martine says - "Maybe, but not now. The disappearance of 9 people among the people, not one of the 1191 people was alive, from ship nothing is stolen, all these things question themselves, why did that ship sink? And now this driver's insurance of 5 crores. And the postmortem report of the remaining 1191 people. There is something wrong......"

At same time a ball gets dropped inside breaking the glass of window.

Martine shouts – "How many times I have told you to play at other place. There is such a big ground in front and everyone is playing in this street."

He picks up the ball, think something and then return it back.

Cherry shocks seeing this and asks – "You have kept all the balls that have come till today but why you return back this ball?"

Martine says with a smile – "These children solved my case."

"How did they solve case?" – Cherry asks.

"We have 1191 people and we are behind 9 people. It means we have whole ground and we are playing in this street only." – Martine says.

Both starts investigation of those 1191 people and then comes a mystery unfolded.

"Oh God, so this is the matter." – Martine says.

"So this means that someone had sunk the ship deliberately. We should inform the CBI" – Cherry says.

Mr. Shekhar Shah of CBI comes to Martine's house. Martine has been working for the government for the 20 years. That's why every government officer recognizes him. And know him because of this courage and passion. And also respect him.

That is why CBI officer Shekhar Shah came to his house himself.

Martine and Cherry put the complete matter in front of him. Shekhar was also stunned.

"How can a person fall so low that he….." – Shekhar thinks.

"This is the list; we will have to gather this entire people this evening." – Martine says Shekhar.

Everyone gathers in the evening around 50-60 people. "On dated 30th April, in Mumbai Arabian Sea a ship was sunk 68 km. from Elephanta, there were a total of 1200 people in that ship, 9 of those are still missing. And rest 1191 people were all killed. Those who died they cannot come back and the 9 people are missing, no clue about them even. There were big celebrities in that 1191. One of them was also Mumbai's biggest businessman." – Shekhar says to everyone.

On hearing his name everyone gets shocked. Because he was a businessman who had decided to donate half of him shares to the blind children's trust.

"Your husband met someone before leaving or something is happened which you felt strange?" Martine asked to the driver's wife of that ship.

"No, I didn't feel anything like this but he used to live very happily." – Driver's wife said.

Then Martine says – "Looking at the whole story, it seems that a ship went into the water and sank due to broken because there were 1200 people aboard this ship and all of them were VIPs. So it was pacified by calling it an accident. But there are some things looking at them it seems that this is not just a coincident, on this route where it has never happened till date that not even gets a chance to escape. Would you all like to know who the murderer is?

"Murderer…?" – Everyone gets shocked.

"Yes murderer, of those 1191 people. That is Mr. George." Martine says pointing to a man standing in the crowd.

That man comes out comfortably from the crowd without fearing, having the smile on face and says – "It seems your mind seems still filled with the water of the sea. That's why you are talking this nonsense."

Cherry says – "It is not any rubbish thing. This is only the truth. You needed money to make more medicines in your factory but Lakshmipati Advani who has been your business partner was not agree now that you make more medicines that too which caused harm. So he decided to donate half of his entire share to the trust. You did not want this to happen. If some happens to Lakshmipati so according to the 'will', the whole business will be yours and the shares that are on his name that too will become yours."

"The story is good but not true. What proof do you have?" – George said.

"There is evidence, this video recording. It is said always that no matter how vicious the perpetrator is, always leaves some clue behind." – Martine says.

Martine shows a picture to George and asks – "Do you know him?"

"No." – George replies.

"If you don't know him then why did you give 5 crores in cash to this man?" – Martine says.

Martine plays a video footage. Cherry pressurizes the George. "Confess the crime. There is no way to escape now. That ship's driver will also be caught soon and there will be no one to save you."

George starts crying and he sits on the chair. And confess everything that – "He did all this for money."

Shekhar asks – "Martine, how did you find it? How did you solve this big case? How did you gather all this evidence? How did you doubt this man among thousands?"

Then Martine explains the whole thing. – "A man, whose salary is 40,000/- rupees, why would he get such an insurance, whose premium will be around 65 thousand every month, 9 people who were missing, when they were investigated, it was found that the driver whose name was Jack Kelly, I and Cherry first suspected him. We went to his house for interrogation. His wife said that everything was normal. There were no tension, no problem. We also talked to people around. His character was also very good. So what happened then that he got such a big insurance done and who gave such a huge amount? We ordered for the video tapes of the intersection near Jack Kelly's house. And this man Mr. George was seen in the same camera giving money to Jack Kelly but the reason was not understood that why did Jack Kelly do this, then I got the thought of human tendency. Greed is one such thing which blinds the great people even. In the greed to earn more Mr. George explained the entire plan by paying money to the Jack Kelly and also got his insurance done. So that he is confident that if anything happens to him even then his family would remain safe. He got tempted. Mr. George gave him amount in cash so that there is no effect on the bank account and no one else should doubt on him. But there was government's record was made of insurance."

"But what was their plan and how did you get suspicious about all this?" – Mr. Shekhar asked.

Martine said - "When the dead bodies were being taken out. Most of the dead bodies were retrieved from the food court of the ship. It shows one thing the ship sank when everyone gathered at the food court together to eat food, around 1191 people because there was also a function after the dinner. But the question arises when the ship started sinking wouldn't anyone have tried to get out of the food court? When I and my team entered the food court, more than half food was swimming there. It simply means that the food of the people was not completed even and the rest of the story was cleared by the postmortem report. Faint medicine was added to all of their food. More than half of the people had eaten, when they became unconscious, the remaining people tried to save them. In that time only one person of Mr. George who was on the board of ship, going to ship's cabinet opened some valves. Due to which water started accumulating rapidly in the ship. Nine people including the driver close the gate and left for their lives and the whole ship sank in water. Faint of the people and so much hustle in the ship, all closed gates; nobody was able to get out. Nobody understood anything. Before anyone could do anything........, so when we opened the room the entire food was swimming, which led to a guess that this incident happened at the time of having meal."

Martine further explained – "Mr. George gave the money and sent some of his other man to get all this done. This man made such a big plan to kill Mr. Lakshmipati Advani, so that nobody is suspicious but made a mistake."

Everyone clapped. Mr. George was arrested. The rest of the people were also caught in a few days.

2 weeks later.......

In the garden in the morning, Martine is working on the laptop, probably writing mail to someone. Cherry comes from behind with the coffee cup.

"What are you doing?" – Cherry asks.

"Just writing one email." – Martine says.

"Email, to whom?" – Cherry asks.

"To Sangeeta Sarkar….. About the box." – Martine replies.

"Box…?" – Cherry gets shocked.

After completion of story Purnima asks – "Box, which box?"

"Hey, are you awake?"

I felt asleep." – Sangeeta said in joke.

"Tell me, which box?" – Purnima asked while hitting the pillow on Sangeeta's shoulder.

"I will not tell" – Sangeeta said laughing jokingly.

"Please tell Sarkar." – Purnima insisted again.

"Okay, I tell you. Listen……….."

Then Sangeeta narrates her one more story.

Chapter 3

Explanation and Realization

There was a small child in a city. He was very naughty, used to have a lot of fun at school and at home, used to fight and quarrel, used to steal someone's pencil and tear someone's book, used to eat someone's tiffin. When he played, he used to start fighting.

His parents were very upset with his habit. They used to scold and beat him a lot but he could not improve. Then his parents took him to a doctor who was a Psychologist.

The doctor asked his parents – "What do you do when he does mischief."

Parent said – "What can we do? We use to scold and beat but he doesn't listen. We have been now upset at all."

Doctor asked - "Why do you scold and beat him?"

The child's mother said – "Sir, last Saturday he was playing cricket with children, when he got out, he wanted to bat again. Just fought with the children on this matter and angrily he did hit the bat at the foot of a child. If he will do so, will he not be beaten? "

The doctor said smiling - "If your child beats someone and if you want to teach him that he should not beat someone but, if you teach this by beating him so you are just convening him the message that fighting is a bad thing. But how to make him realize that he should not do fighting."

The child's father said – "Yes, you are right but what should we do?"

Doctor asked – "Have you ever tried to know if your child does this then why is that the reason?"

The parents bowed their head because they had no answer. Then the doctor explained that – "there is a reason behind any behavior of any human being. Whether he is an older child or a toddler, sometimes mental illness can also occur. Sometimes there can be some stress or an incident in childhood that can have a good or bad affect. We must first understand what the reason behind what is happening is?"

The parents got convinced by doctor's talk. They said to doctor. – "We are now handing over this to you. You have to improve him."

They leave from there.

The child was 8 year old. The doctor did not take long to understand that it was not difficult to make him understand all he was needed the love and care which he could not get due to his parents being busy in job.

After they leave the doctor started looking for his appointment diary but what was, diary was missing, where did it go?

It did not take long for the doctor to understand that it might happen the child had taken that diary but that doctor knew that whatever happens is for good and there is reason behind it. He did not get angry or upset. Rather a smile came on his face and he went to have lunch.

The next day the doctor went to the child's house and talked to him and said that – "will you not take me to show your room?"

The child said in anger – "No."

The doctor smiled and spoke affectionately. See, what I have brought for your room. This poster of spider man, I had to paste it in your room but now as you are refusing then no issue, I will give it to other child.

The child smiled and said. – "No, let paste this in my room only. Let's come to my room."

The child takes the doctor's hand and takes him to his room. When the doctor enters the room he sees posters of many fighters, his room is lying messy. The doctor does not want the fighting posters to be there but he does not intentionally remove them and tells the child - "Your entire walls are full, now where will this spider man get a place."

The child said – "Remove that poster."

The doctor removed the poster of a fighter and pastes a spider man poster there. The child's mother was watching all this. She brought tea and said – "Why are you doing so much?"

Then the doctor said – "I Intentionally removed that fighter's poster, it was inspiring him to fight with people. Now there is a poster of spider man. We have to slowly reduce the things from his room that helps him to get angry and fight."

Mother asked – "But how did you know that he likes spider man?"

The doctor said - "When my assistant was taking his counseling, he himself told that he likes spider man very much and he also finishes his milk due to the spider man and keeps the school copy books arranged in bag because spider man is made on his milk glass and bag."

The mother said – "Yes, that's true."

"The doctor said. If we have to improve anyone or eliminate the evilness of anyone then we should see his goodness not his evilness and his good should be promoted. We should fill the goodness in him. We should give him love so evil ends on its own, just like we light to remove darkness."

The doctor says something in his mother's ear. The mother also smiles and says, - "Yes." And the doctor leaves from there.

In the evening when the child sits to read he does not get a copy and pencil of spider man. He tries to find a lot, even informed to his parents too. Parent also helps him to find it but they do not even get it. At first he is very angry and then starts crying. Cries a lot, his parent leave him in the room and come out.

Father asks his mother – "Somewhere in school itself, he might have forgotten his copy-pencil?"

The mother tells him everything in his ear, the father understands.

The child cries that whole night because it was his very favorite pencil and copy.

The next day, the doctor comes to his home again and brings many more spider man posters and toys. The toys also have a copy and pencil the same, which was missing since yesterday. The child became very happy to see them.

Then he asks to doctor – "Did you take it?"

The doctor says – "Yes."

The child asks with little anger – "Why?"

The doctor says – "You took my diary, didn't you?"

The doctor shows him a video on mobile in which he is keeping the diary in the bag. The child is embarrassed. He goes running and brings the diary he had hidden in his bag to the doctor and also says sorry to him.

His mother has been watching all this. Tears come in her eyes. Gradually that child starts improving and after 6 weeks it shows a lot of change. Now he is not the same as earlier.

The child's parent thanks the doctor and say – "We being parent even, we could not understand how to correct him. He just needed the time love and care which he got from you and also he needed a friend who understands him."

The doctor said - "Giving information (explanation) to someone and making someone realized about something are both different things. Nowadays, parents simply tell to children that what is right and wrong but we should make them realize that what is right and wrong. Only Realization changes the human and for all this it is mandatory to give time to them (children)."

The doctor leaves from there.

After solving this case the doctor takes few weeks' vacation to visit Mumbai at the sea side port.

He finds a ship on which the good are being unloaded. He sees the box from a distance.

A shining box.......

"Again a box, which box and what is in that box?" – Purnima asked with a surprise.

"That, I will reveal you later. Every secret has it is own age and it opens only when the time comes." – Sangeeta says.

"Look, either tell me the secret of this box or narrate me one more story. Think on it." – Purnima puts up a condition.

"Okay, so listen another last story. By this story you will come to know the reason that why any event does happen in life and you will get a positive attitude towards the events." – Sangeeta says.......

Chapter 4

Diamond and King

A king went out hunting in the forest. He went far ahead while hunting. By the midday he gets tired, so after getting off the horse, he starts searching for water reservoir. He is sweating due to the heat. He wipes his sweat by his own stole and also removes the crown. Even when walking long enough, he does not get reservoir so he sits under the shade under a tree. As he sits there he sees something shining under the leaves below. He passes and picks it up. It is a diamond, a very shiny diamond. King keeps it with him and goes head. After going a little distance, he sees a reservoir. He feeds his horse water and also drinks water himself. Then his soul gets some peace. He ties the horse to a tree nearby and he too lies down to rest under the same tree. Then he sees a snake on the tree. He gets scared and gets up quickly and opens his horse from there too and goes ahead. Going forward, he takes out his sword and starts looking for another tree where there is no shake or any other creature. A little ahead he sees a tree and he falls asleep under it. Even at bedtime, he holds the sword in his hand. He sleeps but does not get sleep.

He repeatedly feels that no snake or lion comes. After resting for a while, he goes ahead, walking on foot with his horse. That's when he finds a saint one who was doing penance sitting under a tree. He goes to the saint and salutes them.

Saints say – "come here disciples, king Chaturdhar, how did you get here?"

The king wonders how he knows my name. He says – "Gurudev! How did you know my name? I did not tell you my name.

The saint said- "not only the name Chaturdhar I also know that while coming here you found a diamond and a snake and then you took the whole journey ahead with a sword in hand. Wanted to sleep but could not sleep."

The king was very impressed by his words. He thought that he looked like a very stunning saint, those who have seen everything with their divine vision.

The king asks curiously – "how did you know all this?"

Saint says – "I tell you before that you answer one of my question."

The king said – "Yes, please say Gurudev."

Saint said – “Why did you need that diamond, why did you picked up that diamond what will you do with that? Dear disciple.”

King said that – “I saw something shiny so I was curious. When I saw that, that was a diamond hence, I kept it. Diamond, pearls adorn the kings only. I thought I would put it in my crown.”

Saint said – “But you are the king, you have many diamond gems. Why did you pick up this diamond? You could have thrown it but you have kept it with you. Does doing this suit a king?”

The king was silent. He had no answer.

Then saint said – “Oh Rajan (King), it is not a diamond.”

The king asked with surprise – “What was that then?”

The saint replied that - “I will tell but first tell me what did you do after getting the diamond?”

The king said that – “I was very trusty so I drank water, after that I was sleeping under a tree, then all sudden….”

“…..then all sudden you saw the snake.” – Saint said.

“Yes” – The king said with surprise.

The saint asked – “what did you do then?”

So the king said – "I took out the sword and went a little further to find a place for my rest, I found the place but couldn't sleep."

Then the saint said – "Listen king! It was greed not diamond. When a person has desire to get more than what he needs, it is called greed. You have everything. Your entire palace is filled with diamond beads. You have so much money that even your next seven generations will rule comfortably. Still you picked up that diamond it is not diamond it is greed, king."

The saint said further – "Then when you went ahead, you saw a pond, where you drank water. This meant that after greed the desire of the human mind quenched for a short time then you went ahead and started sleeping under the tree. So you saw the snake and you got scared. It was not the snake, king. It was a fear. When a person had greed in his mind, he quenches his thirst for a short time but he gets scared in his mind. Fear of losing what he has greedily acquired. Then you took out the sword it is a symbol of this that when a man is scared he becomes cruel to protect himself. His intellect becomes corrupt and he takes the path of violence and a violent man never able to sleep peacefully because he is always afraid of being attacked by others."

The saint said further – "Hence, hey king. The reason for the birth of fear is greed. Fear gives birth to violence and violence gives birth to unrest and human being who is (restless) has nothing even after if he has everything because an unquiet (disturbed) human can never lead a happy life and if there is no happiness in life then there is nothing left."

The king places his forehead at the feet of the saint and thanks him for explaining such a great reality of life. The king says – "Hey Gurudev, I would never have received this knowledge, if you had not appeared and I would not have understood that there is a reason behind this incident and whatever happens is also for good."

The saint smiles and says – "But do you know, what was the purpose (reason) behind all this incidents today? Why today you got to learn this, what will you do with this lesson? How will you use this knowledge which I have just given to you?"

The king again became speechless and said – "Gurudev, no I don't know, why all this happened to me today? Tell me please Gurudev."

Then the saint said - "Hey King, in the coming few years you will have a fierce battle with the king of the west. Whenever you do battle after winning it you loot all the wealth of that state and take it to your country. You become the king of that country but what have you done for the people of their till date? You have so much money. If after putting up a war, you will invest the wealth of that king in the wellbeing of the people of that country so you will truly be called a great king. Whatever diamond or pearl you get use it for the good of the people of that country but not to fill your treasure. This will convey the message of not greed among your subjects. If your subjects will not have greed so there will be no fear in them. If there is not fear then there will be no violence between them. If there is no violence, there will be peace. The happiness which will be in your kingdom, this happiness will be the basis of your life.

The king was very happy to hear all this things and he felt that he got the greatest knowledge of life and his life became successful.

He has told the saint – "Hey Gurudev, you have given me such great knowledge, I want to give some gift to you but you are a saint I know that wealth and happiness of the palace is nothing for you. Still I want to give you something in the form of Gurudakshina (Fees). So I promise you that I will do as many wars as I can in the coming times, I will do many such things for the citizens of all those countries that they should not lack anything in my state.

The king goes from there after taking permission from that saint. After few years later he has a battle with the king of the west. He defeats that king but does not loot anything from his kingdom but does a lot of work for the people of that kingdom. He spends all the money for their poverty alleviation and their facilities.

Gradually he becomes a very great and beloved King in times to come.

"Tell me what you understood by this story?" – Sangeeta asked.

"Can I tell you in morning after thinking?" – Purnima said instantly.

"Sure, if you answer correctly, I will reveal the box's secret to you."

"Really…?" – Purnima asks with great curiosity.

"Yes surely. Let's get sleep now." – Sangeeta said.

Purnima agreed. Both switch off the lights and go to sleep.

In the morning Sangeeta informs the Purnima on tea table that, the box was basically of a Golden cover diary of Mr. Lakshmipati Advani. In which he had written a story, actually many stories, which he hid from every one. But now that is another big story, which I will narrate you later in some other time. Purnima also, says, that greed is the reason of fear and then everything bad that happens in life is attached to it.

They both get up from there. Purnima leaves from there. Sangeeta also gets ready and moves out for going to court. It is her the first day of court.

To be continued.........

Most Special Thanks to :-
"GOD"

Special Thanks to My Sisters :-
Shilpa Tai, Swati Tai (Swati Mumma - M.D.), Soumya Tai (Sonmya Mom), Ashwini, Renuka (My Chiku), Swati Khare Tai, Sapna Tai, Sayanti Tai, Vinita.

Special Thanks to Friends :-
"Sangeeta Sarkar", Urwashi Chauhan, Darshan, Honey, Prashant, Mayank Sharma Sir.

Special Thanks to :-
Parents & Family

Sisters: Priyu Tai, Tania Lal (Mah Tanu Tai), Sapna Tai

Friends: Pooja Chouchan, Pragati Chourasiya, Abhishek Prajapati.

Special Thanks to:
My wife Ragini Joshi who helped me to translate this book to English.

The reasons of being "Place"
Cover Designed by:
Ashwini Thatte
Written by: Vishesh Joshi

www.ingramcontent.com/pod-product-compliance
Lightning Source LLC
La Vergne TN
LVHW091223150826
845673LV00003B/989

9798895882856